Bureau of Indian Affairs Law Enforcement Services

Indian Law Enforcement History

PREFACE

Whether it be achieving the peaceful arrest of Geronimo and his heavily armed followers in the 1870's, stopping the liquor traffic in the Indian Territory just after the turn of the century, or maintaining the peace in the emotionally charged atmosphere of the Dakotas in the 1970's, the work of the Indian police has always been challenging. The Indian police carry with them a long and distinguished tradition that provides the inspiration to meet the challenges they face. It extends not merely to the creation of the reservation system, but back into the unrecorded histories of the Native American societies before the white men came.

Many of the men who answered the call to service in the 1870's were already veterans in police work with the police societies of the Plains tribes or the office of High Sheriff of the tribes of the Indian Territory.

Likewise, the first judges selected were often men with distinguished records as leaders of their people. Some, like Quanah and Gall, had been leaders in the fierce Indian resistance to white encroachment. When they saw conditions had changed, they chose again to lead their people and help them make the best of the new world.

This short history of the Indian Criminal Justice system is dedicated to the men and women whose goal it is to carry on this heritage as they work each day to bring the peace, justice and safety so important to the continued development of the communities we serve.

You may notice this document only covers our history up to 1975, and many dramatic changes have occurred since then. When time and resources permit we fully intend to update this section.

Theodore R. Quasula
Director, Office of Law Enforcement Services

Indian Law Enforcement History

A Short History of Indian Law Enforcement

"I have appointed a police, whose duty it is to report to me if they know of anything that is wrong."[1]

With those words Thomas Lightfoot, United States Indian Agent to the Iowa and the Sac and Fox tribes in Nebraska, became the first agent to report the establishment of a Federally-sponsored Indian police in 1869.

Agent Lightfoot's action was his response to a major shift in United States policy toward the Indians. Europeans from the time of their first arrival, had dealt with Indian tribes as sovereign nations. When the Europeans wanted more land, they forced tribes to sign treaties agreeing to move out of the way. When there was no place else to go, the tribes were forced to agree to reserve only a small part of their lands for their own use.

As the white population in Indian country grew, many people began to believe the Government should deal with Indians as individuals rather than as sovereign tribes. Commissioner of Indian Affairs Ely S. Parker expressed this view in 1869 when he urged an end to treaty-making:

> "...because treaties have been made with them, generally for the extinguishment of their supposed absolute title to land inhabited by them or over which they roam, they have been falsely impressed with the notion of national independence. It is time that this idea should be dispelled and the government cease the cruel farce of thus dealing with its helpless and ignorant wards."[2]

Four years later, Commissioner Francis A. Walker recommended a new policy to replace the treaty approach:

> "The reservation system affords the place for thus dealing with tribes and bands, without the access of influences inimical to peace and virtue. It is only necessary that Federal laws, judiciously framed to meet all the facts of the case, and enacted in season, before the Indians begin to scatter, shall place all the members of this race under a strict reformatory control by the agents of the Government."[3]

To implement this policy, Commissioner Walker urged the continued use of the military:

> "Such a use of the military constitutes no abandonment of the peace policy and involved no disparagement of it. It was not to be expected--it was not in the nature of things--that the entire body of wild Indians should submit to be restrained from their Ishmaelitish proclivities without a struggle on the part of the more audacious to maintain their traditional freedom."[4]

There were many persons concerned with Indian Affairs who agreed with Commissioner Walker that Indians should be "reformed" but did not believe the Army should be used to do it. Walker's successor, Edward P. Smith, also urged the use of the military amount the Sioux in his first annual report in 1873.[5] The following year, however, he recommended that deputy U.S. Marshals be used to enforce law among the Indians.[6]

In the meantime, Agent Lightfoot and others improvised their own solutions to the problem. In 1872, Special Indian Commissioner for the Navajos, General Howard, organized a cavalry of 130 Navajos to guard reservation boundaries, arrest thieves and recover stolen stock.[7] The force was successful in recovering 60 head of stock in three months and continued in existence despite orders from Washington that it be disbanded.[8]

In 1874, the San Carlos Reservation Agent, John Clum, wanted to control both the Apaches and the U.S. Cavalry. Clum's predecessors had complained that the reservation was under military control. Agent Clum was determined to change that. he knew he could not assert his independence from the military while depending on it to keep the peace. His answer was to hire four apaches at $15 a month as police. Two months later he asked the military to leave. The military did not oblige, but Agent Clum did manage to function without military assistance.[9] The police force grew to 25 including Clay Beauford, a Virginian he hires as police chief.

The police were establishing themselves in the Plains at the same time. The satisfactory operation of forces among the Winnebago's, and the Santee and Red Cloud Sioux led Commissioner Edward P. Smith to begin encouraging agents to establish Indian police forces. Thirty-nine out of 62 agents favored immediate establishment of forces on their reservation.[10]

There were no funds expressly appropriated by Congress for law enforcement. In 1876, Commissioner John Q. Smith argued for Congressional action in his annual report:

> "Civilization even among white men could not long exist without the guarantees which law alone affords; yet our Indians are remitted by a great civilized government to the control, if control it can be called, of the rude regulations of petty, ignorant tribes."[1.1]

By 1877, the level rhetoric had escalated when Commissioner Ezra A. Hayt quoted Episcopal Bishop William Hobart Hare in his report:

> "Civilization has loosened, in some places broken, the bonds which regulate and hold together Indian society in its wild state and has failed to give people law and officers of justice in their place. This evil continues unabated. Women are beaten and outraged; men are murdered in cold blood; the Indians who are friendly to schools and churches are intimidated and preyed upon by the evil disposed; children are molested on their way to school and schools are dispersed by bands of vagabonds; but their is no redress. The accursed condition of things is an outrage upon the One Lawgiver. It is a disgrace to our land. It should make every man who sits in the national halls of legislation blush. And wish well to the Indians as we may and do for them what we will, the effect of civil agents, teachers and missionaries are like the struggle of drowning men weighted with lead, as long as by the absence of law Indian society is left without a base."[3.2]

The Commissioner asked Congress for funds to pay the police saying:

> "I would recommend that the force be composed of Indians, properly officered by white men, and where capable Indians can be found that they be promoted to command, as reward for faithful service...".

He Noted that such a police force was already working well in Canada and stated:

> "I am thoroughly satisfied that the saving in life and property by the employment of such a force would be very large and that it would materially aid in placing the entire Indian population of the country on the road of civilization."[3.3]

Indian agents did not wait for Congressional action. The agent for the Chippewa's got the tribe to elect policemen who brought offenders before a tribal court of three chiefs. The agent for the Blackfeet was a former city marshal who persuaded the tribe to draft an entire code of laws and create a court to enforce it. At the Spotted Tail Agency in Nebraska, Sioux recruited into the army were available as a police force.[14]

In 1877, the actions of the San Carlos Apache police bolstered the arguments for the Indian police when they peacefully arrested Geronimo and his followers, who were accused of raiding several Arizona settlements. Agent Clum organized a special force of 103 Apaches to make the arrest. Only Clum and 22 policemen went to Warm Springs Agency where Geronimo was. The remainder of the force stayed a few miles out with orders to come in after nightfall. When the reserves slipped in, they were hidden in a commissary warehouse. Geronimo and the 50 men with him believed they had the agent's forces badly outnumbered. But as Clum prepared to make demands, the doors of the warehouse were flung open, and with rifles at the ready, the reserves took control.[15]

Congress appropriated funds for the first time for Indian police for Fiscal Year 1879. The act specified that the $30,000 appropriation was to pay not more than 430 privates at no more than $5 a month and 50 officers at $8 a month. While the available of funds stimulated the rapid growth of the Indian police, the salary limitations provoked cries of anguish from agents throughout the country.[16] Agent Clum had been paying $15 a month for five years.[17] The Indians themselves were well aware that scouts in the Army also received $15 a month.[18] Many agents said they could not recruit a police force at $5 a month.[19] Nevertheless, the Commissioner reported that 30 agency police forces were in existence by the end of 1878 and a code of police rules had been promulgated. He did protest, however, that the salary was adequate only at those reservations where rations were provided.[20]

Duties of the Indian police included arresting and turning back intruders, removing squatters' stakes, driving out cattle, horse or timber thieves, escorting survey parties, serving as guards at ration and annuity distributions, protecting agency buildings and other property, returning truants to school, stopping bootleggers, making arrests for disorderly conduct, drunkenness, wife-beating and theft, serving as couriers, keeping agents informed of births and deaths and notifying agents of any strangers.

> "Vigilant and observant by nature and familiar with every footpath on the reservation."

Indian Law Enforcement History

The Commissioner wrote of the Indian police,

> "No arrivals or departures or clandestine councils can escape their notice, and with a well-disciplined police force, an agent can keep himself informed as to every noteworthy occurrence taking place within the entire limits of his jurisdiction."[21]

The Commissioner also mentioned another aspect of the police system that endeared it to the agents, but provoked violent opposition from many traditional Indian leaders: "The curtailment of prerogatives formerly claimed by tribal chiefs." The Commissioner wrote, "It brings into an agency a new element -- a party which "the idea of the supremacy of law and which by precept and example inculcates that idea in the minds of others of the tribe."[22]

While many traditional Indian communities maintained order without assigning law enforcement responsibilities to specific individuals or groups, many other tribes did have institutions roughly analogous to a police force.

The Chippewa, Creek, and Menominee had rather amorphous police organizations composed of all warriors who had attained a certain minimum distinction in battle.

Among the Osage, the two joint civil head chiefs of the tribe appointed one man from each of the ten clans of the tribe to serve as police in the great bison hunt. The college of seven head civil chiefs of the Omaha appointed a leader of the hunt from one clan and then appointed police to serve under him. The Iowa had permanent police composed of two bodyguards chosen by each of seven civil chiefs. The Pawnee maintained one police force for the village and another for the hunt. Any of seven societies of the Oglala might be called on for policy-duty. The Blackfeet assigned police duties to a particular society only when a special function or occasion made it necessary. Two societies of the Wind River Shoshone held the police function, one of them apparently being superior to the other. Among the Mandan, Arikara policing appeared to be the exclusive prerogative of the Black Mouth society, but among the Crow, nine different societies took turns as police.[23] The Cherokees, because of their long contact with the English, had a police force, called the Lighthorse, which was quite similar to a United States police agency. They also had a court system.

As Agent McGillycuddy of Pine Ridge wrote the Commissioner, traditional leaders understood well the threat that a police force controlled by an agent posed to their authority:

> "The Indians generally recognize the police authority ....From time immemorial there have existed among the Sioux and other tribes, native soldier organizations systematically governed by laws and regulations. Some of the opposition encountered in endeavoring to organize the police force in the spring of 1879 was from these native soldier organizations, for they at once recognized something in it strongly antagonistic to their ancient customs, namely a force at the command of the white man opposed to their own."[24]

Opposition to the establishment of police took several forms. At Colorado River, the agent reported, "The employment of a police has been impracticable, it being unheard of to find a Mohave to denounce another. "[25] At Lower Brule in 1879, a party of about 150 young men under the leadership of one of the chiefs attacked the house and property of the police force, broke the doors and windows and shot their dogs, chickens and hogs. They then forced the police at gunpoint to renounce their promises to serve. [26]

The chief at Rosebud at first opposed the creation of an Indian police, but relented after a visit from the Secretary of the Interior.[27] The police, however, remained loyal to Chief Spotted Tail. During a dispute with agency traders, Spotted Tail ordered the police to keep Indian customers from entering the stores. The police obeyed, much to the consternation of Agent Cook. There was a confrontation between Cook and Spotted Tail during which Cook threatened to organize another police force. After consultations with other Indian leaders, Spotted Tail backed down saying that he had been the agent for his people for so long that he had forgotten his Great Father had sent him one.[28]

A few weeks later, in keeping with his new policy, Spotted Tail reported a horse raid into Nebraska. Captain Crow Dog, accompanied by one white man and eighteen Indian police took the raiders into custody and delivered them to Fort Randall 135 miles away.[29]

Alliances shifted quickly among the Sioux and their agents. Agent McGillycuddy reported, "Enlisted in the police are White Bird and Little Big Man, the latter being a Northern Indian, and having taken a prominent part with Sitting Bull in the Big Horn Campaign of 1878, afterwards surrendering at the Agency with Crazy Horse."[30]

Congress doubled the appropriation and authorized the employment of 800 privates and 100 officers in Fiscal Year 1880, but keep the same pay limits despite the protests of the agents. The following year, the appropriation was raised again to $70,000. By 1881, 49 of the 68 agencies has police.[31] Agent McGillycuddy noted in his 1881 report that the police had maintained quiet among the Oglala for three years. He said the Indian had chosen the Indian police as a lesser evil than the military.[32]

The following year the agent at Lower Brule reported that the Indians now demanded a police force only three years after their attack on the police.[33] The Pima-Maricopa police, however, suffered a severe setback that same year. The Agent allowed the police to leave the reservation to protect some white settlers. The interpreter got drunk and revealed that there were doubts whether funds would be forthcoming to pay the police. The rest of the police then got drunk too and the agent had to reorganize a police force from scratch.[34]

The problems of law enforcement in Oklahoma and the Indian Territory were different from those of the Upper Plains. While the police in the Dakotas were attempting to alter certain aspects of traditional Indian culture, many Indians in the Indian Territory had already adopted many European customs. Police at the Union Agency, serving the Five Civilized Tribes, had to deal with some of the more famous Western outlaw gangs, such as, the Daltons, the Starrs, and the Cooks.

Bob Dalton had once served as Chief of the Osage police until he was fired upon the discovery that he and his brother were bootleggers. They and other members of their family then formed the Dalton Gang and specialized in bank and train robberies until their deaths two years later in Coffeyville.[35]

At times, the gangs threatened to take over entire communities. In 1895, the standing orders of the 40 Union Agency Indian policy read as follows:

> "Arrest all outlaws, thieves, and murderers in your section, and if they resist you will shoot them on the spot. And you will aid and assist all deputy United States Marshals in the enforcement of the law, and make yourself a terror to evil doers."[36]

The Cherokees brought with them from Georgia a complete criminal justice system. Just as agents in the Dakotas recruited members of the tribal police societies to serve on the agency police force, so the Union Agent recruited a former High Sheriff of the Cherokee Nation to be captain of the Agency police in 1880. During his six years in that position, Captain Sam Sixkiller engaged in many gun battles and survived all of those in which he was armed. He was not armed, however, on Christmas Eve, 1886 when he walked out of a drugstore in

Muskogee. Two men stepped out of the darkness armed with a shotgun and .45 pistol. Sixkiller managed to deflect the shotgun blast, but the other man fired four slugs into him. Both killers were captured, but through a combination of escapes and complicated extradition proceedings between the Creek and Cherokee Nations, neither was ever convicted.

The murder caused Congress to pass a law making it a Federal offense to kill an Indian police officer. That law is still in effect and codified as post of 18 U.S.C. 1114. [37]

The most famous shootout involving Indian police occurred three years later when Agent James McLaughlin ordered the Indian police to arrest Sitting Bull in December of 1890. At dawn on December 15, 1890, 39 police officers and four volunteer surrounded Sitting Bull's quarters. The police were inside the cabin before he awakened. he was placed under arrest, but by the time the party was ready to leave, over 100 of Sitting Bull's supporters were gathered outside. Shooting broke out in which Sitting Bull, eight of his supporters and eight Indian police were mortally wounded.[38]

Congress raised the appropriation for Indian police to $82,000 for Fiscal Year 1883 and authorized the employment of 1,000 privates and 100 officers. The following year both funds and employment ceiling were returned to the F.Y. 1882 level. Never again did Congress authorize the employment of as many police as it did in 1883.

Congress, for the first time, allowed a higher police salary in F.Y. 1885 when it authorized the employment of ten Navajo police at $15 a month. The following year it raised the maximum for other police to $8 a month for privates and $10 for officers, but also reduced the employment ceiling by 50 privates and 25 officers. In 1887, the authorized force was again cut by 50 privates and five officers and the special provision for the Navajos was omitted.

On December 2, 1882, Secretary of the Interior Teller sent a memorandum to Commissioner Hiram Price asking him to formulate rules to suppress certain practices that were considered a hindrance to the civilization of the Indians. It was in response to this memorandum that on April 10, 1883, the Commissioner promulgated rules for Courts of Indian Offenses. Agents were instructed to appoint leading tribesmen as judges to act against such practices as sun dancing, medicine-making, polygamy and the sale of wives.[39] Before that time, the agents served as judges. They alone tried and sentenced all Indians arrested by the police.

Commissioner Price requested $50,000 from Congress to pay the judges, but was refused.[40] Faced with the task of implementing the Commissioner's instructions without funds, agents developed two solutions: Some agents appointed members of the police force to be judges since police were already being paid.[41] Other allowed judges to collect their salaried from the fines they levied. The Commissioner scaled down his funding request to $5,000 for 1886, but Congress still refused to appropriate money to pay judges.[42]

Although some agents were very happy to extricate themselves from the unpopular work of ordering punishment for individual Indians, many others were reluctant to initiate the court system. The agent at Rosebud noted, "From the Indian standpoint the offenses set forth and for which punishment is provided are not offenses at all."[43]

The job of policeman involved numerous tasks that were sure to make enemies. They were expected to set an example by wearing white man's attire, cutting their hair, practicing monogamy and taking an allotment. Their duties included determining whether a fellow tribesman was working enough to merit his sugar, coffee, and tobacco rations. As one agent put it. "The police are looked upon as the common foe, and the multitude are bitterly opposed to them."[44] Many agents considered it unfair to ask them without additional pay to take on the even more unpopular job of sentencing their fellow tribesmen.

Although Federally sponsored police and courts were steadily taking over responsibility for internal law enforcement on the reservations, existing statutes and treaties seemed to regard jurisdiction over crimes exclusively involving Indians on Indian land as belonging to the tribe. It was Crow Dog, formerly captain of the police at Rosebud, whose actions brought the attention of the Supreme Court to this issue.

Crow Dog had left the police force and became associated with a faction opposing Spotted Tail. After a tribal council meeting in 1881, Crow Dog suddenly leveled a rifle at Spotted Tail and shot him at point-blank range. Crow Dog was arrested and taken into Deadwood, South Dakota, for trial in Federal Court. He was found guilty and sentenced to death, but was released when the Supreme Court in ex parte Crow Dog, 109 U.S. 556 (1883) held that United States courts had no jurisdiction. The case attracted nationwide attention and pressure for Congressional action. Some Congressmen pushed for extending all Federal law to cover Indians, but others argued that such a move was too drastic. The result was the Major Crimes Act of 1885, now codified as 18 U.S.C. 1153, which gave

Federal Court jurisdiction over acts of murder, manslaughter, rape, assault with intent to kill, arson, burglary and larceny.[45]

The Major Crimes Act was silent on the lesser crimes that were usually brought to the Courts of Indian Offenses. An incident in Oregon brought a measure of Federal judicial sanction to the Indian Courts. The Indian police at Umatilla had arrested a woman for immoral behavior, but she was rescued from the agency jail by friends, who became defendants in the case of U.S. v. Clapox, 35 Federal 575 (1888). When the Federal District Court in Oregon decided the case, it held that Courts of Indian Offenses were "educational and disciplinary instrumentalities, which the United States in its role as virtual guardian of the Indians had the power to create."[46]

Also in 1888, the Courts of Indian Offenses received explicit Congressional sanction when $5,000 was appropriated to pay the judges. That year the judges were paid from $3 to $8 a month, but for seven months only. The next year funding continued at the same level, but in July, 1890, Congress doubled the appropriation. This was done over the objections of Senator Francis M. Cockrell of Missouri, who wanted to hold the line at $75.00. He feared high salaries "...will degenerate into compensation alone, detached from any honor or any respect, simply for the compensation."[47] The Commissioner argued, "The importance, dignity and in many cases unpopularity of the position of Indian judges is such that it should command a salary of at least $10 a month." After the Congressional action, the top monthly salary was raised to $10, but as late as 1925, the standard monthly salary was only $7.

In 1890, the Commissioner wrote, "Without money, legislative authority or precedent these courts have been established and maintained for eight years, and in spite of their crudities, anomalies and disadvantages have achieved a degree of dignity, influence, and usefulness which could hardly have been expected."[48]

Separate funding brought new status to the Indian Courts. In 1890, two former lieutenants of Sitting Bull were on the bench at Standing Rock. One was Gall, a leader at the Battle of the Little Big Horn. The Court meted out sentences from 10 to 90 days at hard labor in the agency guardhouse. That year the Court tried 90 cases, imposed $87 in fines and required 11 offenders to forfeit their weapons.[49]

The Chief Judge at the Kiowa Agency was also a former military leader. Son of a Comanche Chief and a white captive, Quanah Parker was leader of several hundred Plains warriors who launched a dawn attack against the buffalo hunters at Adobe Wells in Texas, the last great battle of the Comanche's. When the Court of

Indian Offenses was first established in 1886, Quanah was names as one of the judges. Two years later he was Chief Judge.[50]

The Kiowa Court file records show several decisions that indicate the Court respected Kiowa and Comanche concepts of justice. There was a manslaughter case involving a person who aimed what he thought was an unloaded gun at a friend when it went off. He received a 10-day jail sentence. A drunk accused of assault received a 4-day sentence. Guilty verdicts in theft cases resulted in one 10-day sentence and two $10 fines. An Indian found guilty of bigamy was ordered to pay the first wife a sum of $10 and to present her with a well-broken pony. In another marital dispute, an Indian accused of seducing a wife was found guilty but not fined or sentenced. The woman involved was ordered to return to her husband and remain with him until his other wife, her sister, had recovered from her current illness.[51]

Quanah Parker's own marital status caused him many problems with Indian Service officials. When he took his seventh wife in 1894, the Commissioner wrote him that he would have to either give her up or lose his judgeship. Quanah signed a pledge saying he would return the seventh wife to her family. But later, after a trip to Washington, Quanah informed the agent that the Commissioner had agreed to let him keep his wife and she subsequently bore him five children. He continued on the bench until 1897 when a new Commissioner heard about his wives and ordered his removal over the vehement protests of the Indian agent.[52]

In 1892, the regulations for the courts were modified so that individual judges were assigned to districts. The court en banc was to be convened only for criminal appeals and civil cases. Judges were authorized to perform marriages.[53] Funding for F.Y. 1892 was raised to $12,540, the highest level it was to reach until F.Y. 1928.

The decision in U.S. v. Clapox left many jurisdictional questions unanswered. The authority of the courts to handle cases involving allottees, whites, mixed-bloods or off-reservation arrests was challenged. The standard Indian Service response was not to press the issue in order to avoid an unfavorable decision.[54]

Some agents allowed judges to be chosen by popular election. Divided into three voting districts in 1892, the Fort Peck Agency was the scene of "electioneering, log-rolling, wire-pulling, and all the etcetera of an election in civilized life," according to the agent. Elections were also held at the Siletz and Crow Creek Reservations.[55]

Fines and hard labor were the most common sentences. In the absence of a jail for the Paiutes in 1888, prisoners were chained to a tree. The usual solution was to convert an extra room at agency headquarters into a cell or to use the guardhouse of an Army post.[56]

The courts made a substantial labor force available to the agents. At the Tulalip Agency in the State of Washington, prisoners were assigned to 600 days of roadwork in 1902. The following year, the figure was 815 days and 1,366 days the year after that. the prisoner was assigned a particular task and it was up to him to get it done before the next session of court. A supervisor would inspect it when the prisoner indicated it was ready.[57]

Funding for the police during this period continued to rise. In 1890, the pay for privates was raised to $10 a month and that for officers to $12 a month. The next year, officer's pay was raised to $15 a month. In 1892, Congress appropriated $156,000. The amount was reduced by $25,400 the next year and stayed below the 1892 level until 1907, when the appropriation was raised to $200,000 and salaries were raised to $20 for privates and $25 for officers.

Despite the increasing funding there were many complaints about the outmoded equipment available to the police. In 1983, the agent at Fort Peck complained that the police were given old Remington revolvers whose cylinders did not revolve. In this report to the Commissioner, he wrote:

> "The idea of ordering a man so armed to arrest a mad Indian who wants to die, but wants to kill as many people as he can before going, and armed with a Winchester rifle. I don't much believe that white soldiers would obey such an order. They should be given the armament, pistol and carbine of the cavalry soldier (caliber .45); and now that this arm is changed by the troops for a more modern weapon a few of these arms in the hands of the Indian police would do as much good for the public in maintaining order as lying piled up in arsenals waiting for a prospective was which may never be realized."[58]

In 1909, Congress added assault with deadly weapon to the list of crimes over which Federal Courts had jurisdiction.

Shortly after the turn of the century, the first Indian policewoman, Julia Wades in the Water, was hired at the Blackfeet Agency in Montana, where she served 25 years. Her assignments included housekeeping and cooking at the jail and handling the women prisoners.[59]

The first general prohibition against liquor in Indian country was passed by Congress in 1832. The liquor laws appear now in much amended form in 18 U.S.C. 1152, 1156, and 1161. For the most part, the Indian police were no match for bootleggers. Most bootleggers were non-Indians. Neither their Indian customers nor their white neighbors willingly gave testimony against them. Deputy U.S. Marshals were assigned to enforcing the liquor laws, but Indian Agents complained that they concentrated on arresting the Indian customers rather than the bootleggers. Many deputies were paid on a fee basis determined by the number of arrests. It was much easier to arrest the customers.[60] Convicting bootleggers was as hard as arresting them. They frequently had good attorneys - as the string of court decisions favorable to the accused attests. Many of the amendments to the liquor law were enacted to plug loopholes discovered by the bootleggers' lawyers. The Justice Department occasionally assigned a special agent to Indian country to stop the more flagrant violations, but the laws continued to be generally ignored. Even the special agent asked that some Indian detectives be hired.[61]

Commissioner William A. Jones first began to ask Congress for funds to gather evidence for prosecuting bootleggers in 1901.[62] His initial request for $10,000 was refused. The request was renewed each year thereafter until Congress relented and appropriated $25,000 for liquor suppression in Fiscal Year 1907. Of that amount, $15,000 was for the Indian Territory.[63]

Shortly after the funds were appropriated, Commissioner Francis E. Leupp reported that he had appointed two Special Officers and would appoint others later. They were called Special officers because they were specialized in enforcement of the liquor laws. "It is hoped by this means," he wrote, "to diminish greatly the sale of intoxicating liquors to Indians."[64] The task would be a formidable one--trying to enforce a very unpopular law in a part of the country not then noted for great respect for laws in general.

The Commissioner assigned William Eugene Johnson to Oklahoma and the Indian Territory. Johnson was a 44-year-old newspaperman. He had gone to college in Nebraska and begun his journalism career there. Later, he became a freelance writer and then an associate editor first of the New York Voice and then the New Voice in Chicago. He was also a strong advocate of prohibition.[65]

Commissioner Leupp wrote, "He was selected for appointment because he had already proved not only his capacity for the sort of work to be demanded of him, but his absolute contempt for danger in the performance of a difficult task." The Commissioner's evaluation was apparently based on Johnson's reputation for plain speaking among people who tended to become violent when they read uncomplimentary stories about themselves. Johnson spent much of his journalism career in courtrooms defending himself against libel suit. According to one report, there were several dents on his bald head that had been made by the gun butts of the plaintiff during a libel trial in Texas.[66]

The first year was a bloody one. Two of Johnson's deputies and ten suspected bootleggers were reported killed.[67]

Although nearly every train into the territory carried whiskey, the express companies generally denied law officers permission to search the cars for evidence. Johnson told the railroad agents that he was willing to take out a search warrant, but if they insisted on it and he subsequently found liquor on their trains, he would arrest them instead of just seizing the contraband. The Commissioner reported, "By degrees, the objections were withdrawn and thus his right to search was recognized...".[68]

Many breweries sold beer with low alcoholic content within the state. Once a market developed, they would increase the percentage of alcohol and boost their sales. Johnson had chemists analyze beer, and they found its alcohol content almost the same as regular beer. He took the reports to four U.S. Attorneys who gave him a written opinion holding the beer to be illegal. He then met with the railroads and persuaded them to issue orders to their agents to refuse shipments from the offending breweries.[69] His agility in dealing with bootleggers won him the sobriquet Pussyfoot, which remained with him the rest of this life.

In 1923, the Native American quoted the following account from the San Bernadino Sun purporting to explain how Johnson became known as Pussyfoot:

> "... he earned the enemy of a dispenser of firewater who swore to kill Johnson on sight. Johnson learned that the dealer did not have an accurate description of him and concluded to face it out. So he went to the joint and called for a drink. The individual behind the improvised bar served him something soft, and Johnson promptly bawled him out, and called for a real drink. Willing to be accommodating, the barkeeper turned to get the ingredients whereupon Johnson reached over and lifted the dealer's two guns out of the holsters and as the amazed individual wheeled about he was looking into the muzzles of his own weapons and very properly and promptly put up his hands, only to be informed this was the Johnson he had sworn to kill. He protested Johnson had

pussyfooted, which pleased the Indians and other border characters to the extent that from that day to this, it was 'Pussyfoot'..."[70]

The Commissioner was lavish in his praise of Pussyfoot Johnson:

"I know of no more efficient officer in the Indian Service; and indeed may safely give him the credit for turning what used to be rather dreary farce into an actual accomplishment in the enforcement of the acts of Congress forbidding the liquor traffic in the Indian Territory."[71]

Another Special Officer, John W. Green, formerly an officer in the Philippine Constabulary, was assigned to the States of Washington and Idaho. Unlike the Indian Territory where it was illegal to import liquor, only sale to Indians was banned in the Northwest. Green visited the bars and secured agreements from them not to sell to Indians. An observer in North Yakima reported that an Indian could scarcely buy a glass of lemonade there after Green came to visit.[72]

The chaotic legal situation resulting from Oklahoma's admission as a State of the Union gave hope to the liquor sellers. During the Months of August, September, and October 1907, the brewers made a concerted effort to overwhelm Pussyfoot with litigation by shipping liquor in from every direction at once and openly operating bars. They had retained more than 20 of the foremost lawyers in the territory to conduct their campaign for them. Frequently, when Pussyfoot or his deputies seized and destroyed malt and fermented beverages, the lawyers for the breweries sued for damages and injunctions. Pussyfoot was arrested four times for "malicious destruction of personal property" to wit, low grade beer. He was once arrested for larceny in seizing and destroying a large amount of whiskey and bar paraphernalia. The malicious destruction cases were dismissed on preliminary examination. In the larceny case, not only was Pussyfoot discharged, but the complainants were bound over to the grand jury. One was later killed in a fight with a deputy. Another was sentenced to the penitentiary for life for killing a man who gave information against him.

The Commissioner reported, "The lively and aggressive contests attending the closing days of the Federal jurisdiction in Oklahoma and the Indian Territory made necessary expenditure of larger sums of money than the regular appropriation would allow and the Congress met the need by making an additional appropriation of $3,500 to complete the year's work."[73]

Indian Law Enforcement History

The appropriation was increased to $40,000 and the liquor suppression office was reorganized on July 1, 1908. Pussyfoot Johnson was named Chief Special Officer with his office in Salt Lake City, Utah, from which he supervised the work of the special officers in the field. "His capacity for such an undertaking long ago passed the experimental stage," the Commissioner wrote.[74]

Pussyfoot did not stay behind his desk. The 1909 Commissioner's Report stated, "In May, Chief Special Officer Johnson visited Laredo, Texas, the source of peyote, bought up the entire supply in the market, destroyed it, and obtained from the wholesale dealers agreements that they would no longer continue in the traffic."[75]

In August 1910, the Superintendent of the White Earth Reservation in Minnesota served formal notice on all saloon keepers in the villages on the Reservation to close their places within 30 days. After the expiration of the 30 days, Pussyfoot and his deputies including his son, Clarence, closed the saloons and destroyed some 1,300 gallons of whiskey. They were later released on a writ of habeas corpus by the United States Federal Court.[76]

At one saloon, a village marshal appeared as he and his deputies were just getting started. Harper's Weekly quoted the following account from the Minneapolis Sunday Tribune:

> "Before the village marshal knew what was happening he was looking into the muzzle of a long, wicked looking revolver which Johnson had suddenly drawn on him. 'I represent the Department of Indian Affairs,' he said quietly, 'I represent the United States Government, and you men had better get out of here until we finish our work.' The men demurred and the village marshal became insistent. Suddenly smiling Johnson became transformed. 'Get our of here', he thundered, advancing a step in the direction of the frightened marshal and his posse, and they accepted the spirit of the invitation."

After he completed his work, Johnson with his gun holstered now, went up to the marshal and asked him if he wanted to arrest them. The marshal said he did and Johnson and his deputies went off quietly to jail.[77]

The 1855 Treaty by which the Chippewa's ceded much of Minnesota to the United States contained a provision that liquor would not be sold in the ceded territory. The Special Officers attempted to enforce the Treaty. That action provoked a strong reaction since two-thirds of Minnesota and the City of

Minneapolis are within the ceded area. A brewery in Bemidji obtained an injunction against enforcement of the Treaty claiming the treaty provision had been repealed by the Minnesota Enabling Act, which permitted Minnesota to enter the Union on "an equal footing" with other States.[78]

Pussyfoot resigned on September 30, 1911, after securing more than 4,000 liquor law convictions. He quickly became a leader in the world-wide prohibition movement. He circled the globe three times and made over 4,000 speeches supporting prohibition. Although he came through his battles as Special Officer unscathed, he was not so fortunate when he took his campaign to London. A group of medical students mobbed him during an anti-alcohol speech in Essex Hall in 1919 and stones were thrown at him. One stone struck him in one eye and ultimately blinded him in that eye. The students carried him through the streets of London on a stretcher chanting, "We've got Pussyfoot now, send him back to America." Interviewed later in his hospital bed, Pussyfoot said that aside from the injury to his eye he thoroughly enjoyed the experience.[79]

Pussyfoot was succeeded by Harold F. Coggeshall, who stayed only a few months before being named Superintendent of the Santa Fe Indian School. Reverend C.C. Brannon was Acting Chief Special Officer for a few months before Henry Larsen was appointed. In 1910, the headquarters had been moved to Denver. Larsen asked his officers to enforce Minnesota state law against selling liquor to Indians while the Chippewa Treaty was tied up in litigation. This was not very successful since Minnesota law forbade the use of undercover agents. Back in Washington, D.C., the commissioner reported that one conviction for selling liquor to an Indian was secured in the Nation's Capitol.[80]

Commissioner Robert G. Valetine himself ran afoul of the liquor law when he was accused of taking a bottle of liquor with him to the Osage Reservation in Oklahoma. The incident provided one of the many charges raised against the Commissioner by a Congressional investigating committee.[81]

The new Commissioner, Cato Sells, issued an order to all employees not to use liquor on the reservation--even for medicinal purposes. The following year he attended the second annual conference of Special Officers in Denver.[82]

Some favorable court decision enabled Special Officers to step up their activities in Oklahoma in 1913. The work was still very dangerous. Officer P.L. Bowman was killed by a shotgun blast from a speeding car at the Kansas border while he was destroying a wagon load of liquor.[83]

When the Special Officer force was first created in Fiscal Year 1906, the officers had been given the powers of Indian agents, including the authority to seize and destroy contraband. The 1913 Appropriation Act conferred upon Special Officers the powers of U.S. Marshals. The Marshals had the same powers as the sheriff of the jurisdiction in which they were working.

During 1913, the courts held that the making of tiswin, a local Arizona Indian alcoholic beverage, violated the liquor laws. The Special Officers, however, were not very effective in suppressing tiswin because it did not have to be imported. The liquor law was amended to allow wine to be brought into Indian country for sacramental purposes. The same year the Indian Services announced a policy of prosecuting peyote traffickers.[84]

In 1914, the appropriation for liquor suppression was increased by $25,000 permitting a raise in pay for the Special Officers. Activities increased in New Mexico with a court decision declaring that Pueblos were Indians.[85]

It was 1915 before the Bemidji (Minnesota) brewery case, Johnson v. Geralds, 234 U.S. 422 (1914), was decided by the Supreme Court in the Government's favor. As soon as the injunction was lifted, the Special Officers destroyed 745 barrels of beer at the Bemidji Brewery Company.[86]

In 1912, the Indian judges appeared to lose favor with Congress. The judicial appropriation was cut by $2,000 for F.Y. 1913 and reduced another $4,000 in F.Y. 1914 to $8,000. Bureau officials continued to characterize the courts as schools for teaching Indians right from wrong. The courts were also justified on the grounds that having Indians judging Indians removed the possibilities that racial prejudice would become involved in judicial decisions.[87] The total number of judges dropped from 126 in 1912 to 85 in 1919. The reduction was accomplished by reducing most of the three-judge panels to one judge.[88]

In F.Y. 1917, the liquor suppression budget was increased by $50,000 because recent court decisions had given the Bureau more responsibility in Oklahoma.[89]

The increase brought the total Bureau of Indian Affairs law enforcement budget to a record $358,000. The appropriation stayed at this level for three years when the advent of National Prohibition led to a steady decline in the liquor suppression budget. Bureau of Indian Affairs law enforcement funding did not again equal the 1917 level until 1955.

The trend was also downward in the number of Indian police. In 1912, there were 660 police officers.[90] By 1920, there were 548 even though the appropriation remained at $200,000.[91] Then an economy drive hit the police. The F.Y. 1922 budget was cut to $150,000 and the police force was reduced to 361 officers. The Bureau reported that the police were allowed to farm so they could survive on the meager salary.[92] Another $1,000 was cut from the judicial appropriation in F.Y. 1921. The cuts continued through F.Y. 1925 when the police appropriation was $125,000 and only $6,500 were provided for judges. The police force dropped to 271 officers. Only 70 judged remained by 1926.[93]

Because of National Prohibition the liquor suppression office suffered more drastic cuts. In 1918, there had been in addition to the chief special officer, one assistant chief special officer, 17 special officers and 95 deputies.[94]

By 1921, there remained only the chief special officer, four regular special officers and an unspecified number of deputies paid at the rate of $4 a day.[95] The appropriation bottomed out in 1926 at $22,000. In the leaner years, the fines paid by people arrested by liquor suppression personnel were more than the appropriation.[96]

The position of the Courts of Indian Offenses was strengthened somewhat by the passage of the Snyder Act (25 U.S.C. 13) in 1921. Prior to that year, Congress had appropriated funds for the activities of the Bureau of Indian Affairs without giving the Bureau explicit and permanent authority to spend it. The Snyder Act gave the Bureau of Indian Affairs that authority. The Act specifically stated that funds could be spent for the employment of Indian judges. Although the Act did not spell out the jurisdiction of these judges, it did give a clear indication that Congress meant for Courts of Indian Offenses to exist.

Three years later, however, Congress passes a law making all Indians American citizens. Although the old U.S. v. Clapox decision had upheld the validity of the courts, the Bureau had always avoided litigation involving Indians who had become citizens, now it would be difficult to avoid such a test without giving up the courts entirely.

In the Spring of 1926, hearings were held on H.R. 7826, an administration-backed Bill to spell out the jurisdiction of the Courts of Indian Offenses. The Bill would have applied all Federal law to Indians on reservations. Courts of Indian Offenses would have been granted jurisdiction to punish acts not punished by Federal law. The sentencing power of the Indian Courts would be limited to six months and a $100 fine. The Act would also abolish custom marriages and divorces.[97]

Much of the hearing was a debate over the past performance and usefulness of the Indian Courts. The tribes were divided on the issues. The Pueblos and some California tribes were opposed, but many of the tribes in the Northern Plains supported the Courts.[98] John Collier, later to become Commissioner under President Franklin Roosevelt, was a champion of those opposed to the legislation. He argued that the judges were puppets of the superintendents and that administrative officials should not have so much power. He said the Courts provide no due process and no appeal. He argued they represent a government of men not of laws.[99]

Jennings C. Wise, a Washington lawyer for many Indian groups, argued the Bill was unconstitutional because it would provide courts that would send people to jail for violating mere regulations. He believed that adjudication by an executive agent could not be considered due process. He noted that the legislation provided for no grand or petit jury contrary to Constitutional requirements. Since the proposed legislation was largely designed to authorize the existing practice, Wise was by implication arguing that the existing Courts were unconstitutional.[100]

Proponents argued the Courts were needed since only eight crimes were covered by the Major Crimes Act and tried in Federal court. They felt State and Federal Courts tended to be too far from the reservation to handle the bulk of lesser criminal offenses. The Bureau noted that there was a provision for appeal of a court's decision first to the Superintendent and then to the Commissioner of Indian Affairs. Proponents also pointed to the fact that cases could be tried in the native language of the accused in Indian Courts.[101]

Collier proposed alternatives which were embodies in H.R. 9315 sponsored by a Wisconsin Congressman. That Bill would provide for Commissioner nominated by the tribe and appointed by the Federal Courts. Appeals could be taken from decisions by the Commissioners directly to the Federal District Court.[102]

There was also a lively debate on the matter of abolishing custom marriages and divorces. Father Ketcham, of the Board of Indian Commissioners, supported abolition because he said younger Indians who were otherwise assimilated used the institution of custom marriages and divorces to avoid punishment for promiscuity.[103] Collier argued that abolition would just make criminals out of many Indians.[104]

Neither Bill passed Congress although some of the concerns expressed during the hearing were later addressed by the Indian Reorganization Act, amendments to the Major Crimes Act, the Indian Civil Rights Act and a 1956 Eighth Circuit Court decision.

The Bureau asked for major increases for both police and judges for F.Y. 1926. Congress had recently passed a salary reclassification act and the Bureau believed both the police and the judges should be included. The judicial request was $20,000 -- more than triple the existing appropriation -- to enable judges to be paid $20 a month. Instead, Congress raised the amount to $8,400 so judges could be paid $10 a month. The Bureau of Indian Affairs request of $190,000 for police was reduced to $177,760 -- still an increase of more than $50,000 over the F.Y. 1925 amount.

Some Congressmen wondered whether the police budget might not be reduced if the practices of using police for carrying messages, serving as janitors and performing other non-enforcement duties were ended. A Bureau of Indian Affairs spokesman replied, "If it were not for the services rendered by these police, it would be necessary for us to employ white people to render the service at much higher compensation."[105] The pay differential was apparent even within the Bureau of Indian Affairs law enforcement field. In 1932, for example, the top pay for an Indian chief of police was $840 a year compared to the salary for a Bureau of Indian Affairs deputy special officer of $1,800.[106]

Members of the appropriation committee asked the Bureau of Indian Affairs to tell them which judges had the heaviest workloads so a pay scale could be established. The Bureau named 32 courts -- mostly in the Dakotas and Arizona -- where the workloads justified higher salaries.[107] For F.Y. 1928, Congress raised the appropriation committee's recommendation for judges from $8,400 to $15,000. The increase went to those 32 courts to raise the salaries to $25 a month. Two years later, Congress added another $3,000 to give all judges a $5 a month raise.

In 1929, the Bureau was able to convince Congress that the Federal agents assigned to enforce National Prohibition were not adequate to enforce the Indian liquor laws. The Bureau pointed out that the many special laws and treaties were involved on Indian reservations. In general, it was found that it was easier to get a conviction under the Indian liquor laws and treaty provision than under the Volstead Act.[108] $100,000 was appropriated for F.Y. 1930 and the force increased from six to 18 officers including Chief Special Officer N.J. Folsom whose headquarters' was Sioux Falls, South Dakota. Prior to his promotion, he had been working as Special Officer, primarily at Turtle Mountain. The most serious liquor laws problems were on the Menominee and Navajo Reservations and in Montana.

Indian Law Enforcement History

Many Indians who were unable to get regular alcoholic beverages had begun to use canned heat.[109]

Two more offenses were added to the Major Crimes Act of 1932. The Bureau asked that the crimes of incest, robbery, carnal knowledge, attempted rape and assault with intent to do great bodily harm be added to the list of offenses tried in Federal Court, but Congress added only incest and robbery.

The Fiscal Year 1933 budget was the first to reflect depression belt tightening. The $3,000 increase the judiciary received in 1930 was taken back and the police budget was cut by $13,000. The top judicial salary was cut to $25 a month. The F.Y. 1935 budget contained more drastic reductions. While the judges sustained only a 10 percent reduction, the police lost $44,000. Eighty police position were abolished and the pay of those remaining was cut by 15 percent. The liquor suppression budget was cut in half leaving only six special officers and four deputies.[110] Although the budget began to grow again in F.Y. 1936, it did not return to the F.Y. 1932 level until F.Y. 1951. Federally funded law enforcement staffing did not reach the F.Y. 1932 level again until F.Y. 1959.

One of the many changes proposed by Commissioner John Collier in 1934 was a plan for a national Indian judicial system. Title IV of the Indian Reorganization Bill would have created a Court of Indian Affairs with a chief justice and six associate justices. The criminal jurisdiction would include all violations of Federal law in Indian country regardless of whether or not the accused was Indian. The proposal was strongly criticized from many quarters and was dropped from the bill.[111]

Portions of the Indian Reorganization Act did become law, the Constitutions were adopted by the tribes and tribal governments were organized. Many of the new organizations included tribal courts. Some even established a tribal police department. Tribes were also able to enact their own penal code with the approval of the Secretary of the Interior. The tribal code, once adopted and approved, replaced the Bureau of Indian Affairs issued regulations governing Indian offenses as the law for the tribe adopting the new code. Fines levied in the tribal courts were used to pay incidental expenses incurred by the court.

After the death of the Chief Special Officer N.J. Folsom in 1932, Louis C. Mueller was named to the post. For a few months in the winter of 1933, the headquarter was in Carson City, Nevada, but was then moved to Denver, Colorado. Mr. Mueller had previously served as Special Officer at Klamath Falls, Oregon. Tribal funds had paid his salary there. He had been responsible not just for liquor suppression but for all law enforcement there.[112] As the appropriation began to rise again, Mr. Mueller assigned some Special Officers to reservations to serve as Chiefs of Police. Commissioner Collier told Congress this move helped to develop more efficient police departments, better trained in the law of arrest and general criminal investigation. Some Indian police were promoted to better-paying Agency Special Officer positions. By the end of Collier's term as Commissioner, about half of the Special Officers were Indians.[113]

A strong defender of freedom of worship for the Native American Church, Collier asks Congress to drop peyote from the liquor suppression appropriation. He stated that peyote is no more dangerous than the sacramental wine permitted under the liquor laws. Congress agreed to delete mention of peyote from the F.Y. 1930 appropriation. He asked that the separate appropriations for police, judges and liquor suppression be consolidated, but Congress did not accede to this request until F.Y. 1938.[114]

Roosevelt's economic recovery programs created some additional law enforcement problems by bringing additional income into the reservations, which increased liquor consumption and alcohol-related crime. At the same time, however, the Indian Emergency Conservation Work program included 20 positions for policemen.[114] This program continued until after the start of the Second World War.

The repeal of National Prohibition made judges more willing to convict violators of Indian liquor laws. The conviction rate was about 88 percent. Although the narcotics situation seemed to be improving in Nevada, it was getting worse in Oklahoma.[116]

In 1937, approximately $50,000 was still used for liquor suppression officers who worked throughout the nation.[117]

Many characteristics of the Indian criminal justice system remained as they were at the turn of the century. Jails were still so inadequate that judges rarely committed anyone to them except to sleep off a drunk. The usual sentence was a few days of labor.[118] The pay continued at a very low level. "We would have to pay a much larger salary for white police," one BIA official told an appropriation subcommittee in 1939.[119]

The Second World War saw a continued slow decline in law enforcement staffing. From 1940 to 1946, the number of Bureau of Indian Affairs funded judges dropped from 67 to 58. The number of police dropped from 171 to 146 during the same period.[120]

These reductions prompted a few tribes to continue their courts by paying their own judges. The availability of well-paying jobs in defense plants made it more difficult to keep law enforcement personnel.[121]

In 1942, the remainder of the Special Officer force was assigned to the reservations, but many still concentrated their efforts on liquor law violations.[122] The policy was established of trying Indians accused of liquor law violations in tribal courts unless the amount of liquor involved indicated commercialism or unless the accused had a long record of previous liquor law violations. There also developed a tendency for the United States Attorneys to refer minor larceny cases to the Indian Courts. On many reservations, however, only the crimes mentioned in the Major Crimes Act were prosecuted because the Indian Courts no longer existed.[123]

By 1947, there were 31 Special Officers paid with Federal funds. Tribes paid the salaries of another nine Special Officers. That same year the 58 Indian judges were given a big raise. The highest paid judges received a $120 a year increase to bring them to $900 a year. The lowest paid judges received a $300 increase bringing their yearly salary to $480.[124]

The next year, however, only 13 of those judges were still on the payroll. Termination fever came early to Bureau of Indian Affairs law enforcement. The F.Y. 1948 budget was slashed to $12,940--less than half of the appropriation for the previous year. Forty-five police--less than a third of the force the year before--remained on the Federal payroll.

Tribal governments, while complaining bitterly about the cuts, moved to take up some of the slack. In 1948, tribal funds paid for seven Special Officers, two Deputy Special Officers, 15 policemen and three judges.[125]

The Bureau asked Congress to restore the budget to the F.Y. 1947 level, but instead the House recommended that law enforcement be eliminated from the budget entirely in F.Y. 1949 leaving the job to the states. The Senate, while expressing sympathy with the idea, concluded the appropriation had better be continued until legislation was passed giving jurisdiction to the states.[126] After Senate action, the appropriation contained a slight increase over the F.Y. 1948 level. The next year the appropriation was increased another $50,000--still well below the F.Y. 1947 amount.

By 1950, the effect of the drastic cuts were clear. Senator Gurney spoke of one reservation community in his South Dakota district.

> "They cannot have a dance at night because there is so much disorder. There is nobody to control the peace of that community and there is so much disorder they just do not have any community gatherings at night. It is impossible and I wrote Commissioner John R. Nichols a letter and told him about the need for law and order in the Rosebud and Pine Ridge Reservations. I have not had an answer. I am expecting him to tell us what we need out there. It is terrible. There are four or five murderers that have not been apprehended."

Commissioner John R. Nichols told the Senator that the situation in his state existed throughout Indian country. "This is the lowest point in the history of law and order." Nichols said, "We haven't even a person in the Washington office who devotes full time to law and order. We haven't got a single Special Officer in the Washington office whom we can send to investigate a crime, bootlegging, murder or anything else."

The Bureau of Indian Affairs had asked for 20 new positions and $86,065 in additional funds for F.Y. 1951. Senator Gurney asked if that was all the Bureau needed.

The Commissioner returned with a request five times the size of the existing appropriation. A major portion of the request was to fund programs currently supported by the tribes. By this time tribes were spending $300,000 a year on law enforcement. The request asked for a total of 48 Special Officers -- eight in Area Offices and 40 assigned to reservations. At that time only the Billings, Phoenix, Portland and Minneapolis Areas had Special Officers assigned to them. Another five Special Officers would work in Navajo border towns. There would be 45 more Indian judges in addition to the existing 12. The requests would provide for 123 more police, 53 court clerks, 34 jailers and 37 other jail personnel such as, janitors and cooks. Congress granted an 80 percent increase over the previous year's amount.[127]

With the partial restoration of the funding, Mr. William Benge, a reservation Superintendent in New York, was named Chief Special Officer with Washington, D.C. as his headquarters. A few months later he was named Chief of the Branch of Law and Order with responsibility for all aspects of the BIA's criminal justice activities. Previously, matters concerning the Indian police and the judges were handled by other branches. The Branch of Education had the assignment in the

Indian Law Enforcement History

early part of the century, the responsibility was later moved to the Branch of Welfare.

In 1953, the Indian termination drive manifested itself in substantive legislation. Public law 83-277 limited the Indian liquor laws to Indian country. Before, it had been illegal to sell liquor to Indians anywhere in the United States. Within the reservations, local options were made available where state laws would permit.

During the period 1953-1970, a large number of Indian tribes and similar groups, through Congressional enactments, had their Federal trust relationships terminated. These actions subjected such tribal members and their reservations to State criminal and civil jurisdiction, if by some other Congressional enactment; they had not been previously made subject to such jurisdiction. The following Indian tribes or similar groups terminated are as follows:

Name	Authorizing Statute	Effective Date
Alabama and Coushatta Tribes of Texas	68 Stat. 768	7-1-1955
Catawba Indians of South Carolina	73 Stat. 592	7-1-1962
Klamath and Modoc Tribes and the Yahooskin Band of Snake Indians (Oregon)	67 Stat. 718	8-13-1961
Mixed-blood Ute Indians of the Uintah and Ouray Reservation (Utah)	68 Stat. 724	8-27-1961
Ottawa Tribe of Oklahoma	70 Stat. 963	8-3-1959
Peoria Tribe of Oklahoma	70 Stat. 936	8-3-1959
Paiute Indians of Utah (Indian Peaks Band, Kanosh Band, Koosharem Band and the Shivwitz Band of Paiute Indians	68 Stat. 1099	3-1-1957
Ponca Indian Tribe of Nebraska	76 Stat. 429	10-27-1966

Indian Law Enforcement History

Tribes and Bands of Oregon including the following tribes, bands, groups or communities of Indians: Confederated Tribes of the Grande Ronde Community, Confederated Tribes of Siletz Indians, Alsea, Applegate Creek, Calapooya, Chaftan, Chempho, Chetco, Chetlessington, Chinook, Ckackamas, Clatskanie, Clatsop, Clowwewalla, Coos, Cow Creek, Euchees, Galic Creek, Grave, Joshua, Karok, Kathlamet, Kusotony, Kwatami or Sixes, Lakmiut, Long Tom Creek, Lower Coquille, Lower Umpqua, Maddy, Mackanotin, Mary's River, Multnomah, Munsel Cree, Naltunnetunne, Nehalem, Nestucca, Northern Mollalla, Port Oxford, Pudding River, Santiam, Scoton, Shasta, Shasta Costa, Siletz, Siuslaw, Skiloot, Southern Molalla, Takelma, Tillamook Tolowa, Tualatin, Tututui, Upper Coquille, Upper Umpqua, Willametta Tumwater, Yambill, Yaquina and Yoncalla	68 Stat. 724	8-13-1953

California Individual Rancheria Acts:

Name	Authorizing Statute	Effective Date
Coyote Valley	71 Stat. 283	1957
Laguna	61 Stat. 731	1958
Lower Lake	70 Stat. 58	1956

California Rancheria Act as Amended via 72 Stat. 691 & 76 Stat. 390

Name	Effective Date
Alexander Valley (Wappo)	8-1-1961
Auburn	12-30-1965

Indian Law Enforcement History

Big Valley (Pinoleville)	11-11-1965
Blue Lake	9-22-1966
Buena Vista	4-11-1961
Cache Creek	4-11-1961
Chicken Ranch (Jamestown)	8-1-1961
Chico (Meechupta)	6-2-1967
Cloverdale	12-30-1965
Crescent City (Elk Valley)	07-16-1966
Graton (Sebastopol)	02-18-1966
Greenville	12-08-1966
Guidiville	09-03-1965
Indian Ranch	09-22-1964
Lytton	08-01-1961
Mark West	04-11-1961
Mooretown	08-01-1961
Nevada City	09-22-1964
North Fork	02-18-1966
Paskenta	04-11-1961
Picayune	02-18-1966

Indian Law Enforcement History

Pinoleville	02-18-1966
Potter Valley	08-01-1961
Quartz Valley	01-20-1967
Redding (Clear Lake)	06-20-1962
Redwood Valley	08-01-1961
Robinson (East Lake)	09-03-1965
Rohnerville (Bear River)	07-16-1966
Ruffeys (Ruffeys Valley - Etna Band)	04-11-1961
Scotta Valley (Sugar Bowl)	09-03-1965
Smith River	07-19-1967
Strawberry Valley	04-11-1961
Table Bluff	04-11-1961
Wilton	09-22-1964
Shingle Springs (Verona tract)	07-16-1966
Mission Creek	07-14-1970
Strathmore	08-16-1967

Public Law 83-280 conferred criminal and civil jurisdiction over Indian country to the States of California, Minnesota, Nebraska, Oregon and Wisconsin with the exceptions of the Red Lake Reservation in Minnesota, the Warm Springs Reservation in Oregon and the Menominee Reservation in Wisconsin. The same act also gave consent to other states to assume jurisdiction over Indian country by

State Constitutional amendment or legislative action. Jurisdiction was conferred on Alaska when it became a State. An exception was made later for Metlakatla when legislation was passed in 1970 giving the Indian community concurrent jurisdiction over minor offenses. Florida assumed complete jurisdiction under the Statute.

The Menominee's of Wisconsin were brought under the act in 1954. In 1944, Nevada enacted law which assumed civil and criminal jurisdiction by the State over all Indian country within the State. However, it provided that within 90 days after July 1, 1955, the county commissioners of any county could petition the Governor to exclude the Indian country in that county from the operation of the act. Eight of the sixteen counties involved chose to continue Federal jurisdiction.

Montana enacted legislation for the Flathead Reservation covering felonies and providing concurrent jurisdiction for misdemeanor offenses and certain civil matters.

Washington enacted legislation first in 1957 so that tribes could go under State jurisdiction voluntarily and in 1963 assumed partial jurisdiction over all reservations in the State.

In 1963, the State of Idaho extended partial jurisdiction, on a concurrent basis, to Indian country in the State and made provisions so a tribe could come under full jurisdiction of the State.

Prior to enactment of Public Law 83-280 in 1953, Congress had, through legislation, granted jurisdiction, under certain conditions, to the States of Kansas (18 U.S.C. 3243), and North Dakota (60 Stat.229). However, the statute relating to jurisdiction of North Dakota was found to be unconstitutional by the State Supreme Court and was never implemented.

Hearings by the Senate Judiciary Committee on juvenile delinquency problems in North Dakota produced a recommendation in 1955 that the Bureau of Indian Affairs criminal justice budget for the State be increased from $15,000 a year to $276,000. The same year the BIA estimated $1,465,000 would be needed to do a totally adequate job.

For F.Y. 1956, the Bureau of Indian Affairs had asked the House of Representatives for the same amount as the year before. Buoyed by the findings of the judiciary committee, however, the Bureau asked the Senate for $800,000 --

Indian Law Enforcement History

more than double the existing funds.[128] Congress appropriated $400,000 which was still a substantial increase over the F.Y. 1955 amount.

The Bureau returned the following year and asked both Houses to double the appropriation. Bureau of Indian Affairs officials pointed out that the ratio of police to residents on Indian reservations was two per 5,000 population compared to a rate of ten per 5,000 in the country as a whole.

They said the various efforts by the Congress to reduce the jurisdiction and; therefore, the workload of the Indian police, had not had the desired effect. The relaxation of the liquor laws brought more drinking and more alcohol-related crimes. Already 28 tribes had voted to legalize alcoholic beverage under the new local option provisions. Few additional stated were assuming jurisdiction under Public Law 83-280. State authorities' were reluctant to assume jurisdiction without Indian consent and few tribes would give their consents. Many tribes considered the maintenance of tribal and Federal jurisdiction essential to their treaty rights.

The police force, now with 65 officers, still had not recovered by 1956 from the drastic cut in F.Y. 1948. A Bureau of Indian Affairs official said, "In recognition of our inability for lack of funds to fulfill law and order needs, every effort has been made to encourage those tribes with financial resources to assume increased responsibility for these activities on the reservation."[129] Congress granted the full request.

In 1956, the Eighth Circuit Court of Appeals resolved the question of whether a United States citizen could be subject to an Indian court. In Iron Crow v. Oglala Sioux Tribe, 231 F. 2d 89 (8th Cir. 1956), the Court spoke directly to the issue:

> "...It would seem clear that the Constitution, as construed by the Supreme Court, acknowledges the paramount authority of the United States with regard to Indian tribes but recognizes the existence of Indian tribes as quasi sovereign entities possessing all the inherent rights of sovereignty excepting where restrictions have been placed thereon by the United States itself.

The Court went on to say:

> "That Congress did not intend by the granting of citizenship to all Indians born in the United States to terminate the Indian Tribal Court system is patent from the fact that at the same session of Congress and at sessions continuously subsequent thereto funds have been appropriated for the maintenance of the

> Indian Tribal Courts. We hold that the granting of citizenship in itself did not destroy tribal existence or the existence or jurisdiction of the Indian Tribal Courts and that there was no intention on the part of the Congress so to do."

By finding that the authority of Indian Courts derives from Indian sovereignty rather than the power of the United States, the court succeeded in putting the courts on a much firmer base. The old Clapox decision had upheld the courts only as "educational and disciplinary instrumentalities."

For F.Y. 1958, an increase of $63,000 was obtained to improve prison facilities. The University of South Dakota law school began a training program for Indian judges.

The budget passed the million dollar mark for F.Y. 1960 when another $300,000 was added to hire 23 more employees in the Aberdeen and Phoenix Areas.[130]

Some tribes began to feel the strain of funding their own law enforcement programs. By 1961, the Bureau of Indian Affairs was paying for 45 special officers, 61 police, 17 judges and 20 other employees working in the jails and courts. Tribes, on the other hand, were paying for 331 police, 30 jail attendants, 74 judges and ten other judicial employees. Tribes at all but four reservations paid at least part of the law enforcement costs.[131]

With the F.Y. 1963 budget proposal, the Bureau began a series of requests for funds to take over programs operated by the tribes. Over the next three years more than a million dollars was added to the law enforcement appropriation and more than 100 additional law enforcement employees were added to the BIA payroll. Much of these new funds went to relieve tribes of law enforcement funding responsibilities.

A substantial portion was also used to mount a rehabilitation effort. Probation and juvenile officers were employed on the reservations. At the height of the program in F.Y. 1964, there were 50 probation and juvenile officers employed.

The probation officers worked under the supervision of the Agency Special Officer. Most special officers chose to hire additional enforcement and jail personnel whenever a probation officer resigned. Since then, the number of probation and juvenile officers has declined to less than ten.

By the mid-1960's, more emphasis was being placed on training. Adult Vocational Training funds were used to train the Indian police. Special Officers attended summer training courses at law schools.[132]

The Bureau continued during this period to obtain funding increases to permit assumption of the financial burden of law enforcement that tribes had been carrying. One major exception; however, was the Navajo Tribe. By 1966, the tribe's own law enforcement budget had grown to $2,000,000. The Navajo judiciary has undergone an extensive training program recommended to them by the Honorable Warren E. Burger, Chief Justice of the United States Supreme Court.[133]

After Mr. Benge's retirement in 1969, Eugene F. Suarez, Sr., Special Officer at the Salt River Reservation in Arizona, was named Chief of the Branch of Law and Order.

The law enforcement justification for F.Y. 1969 was an unprecedented 22 pages long. Statistics of crime in the United States as a whole were compared with the reservation crime rates. Data were presented on repeated offenders and jail facilities. Of the $2,100,000 increase requested, Congress granted one million dollars. Some of the funds were used to start three new programs: (1) The Indian Police Academy; (2) The Indian Offender Rehabilitation Program; and (3) Reservation Rehabilitation Centers.

In 1969, the Police Academy was established in Roswell, New Mexico, and operated under contract by the Thiokol Company. The Academy offered basic police training courses for BIA and tribal police. By 1971, additional training courses were added for juvenile officers and criminal-investigators. In 1973, the Indian Police Academy was relocated to Brigham City, Utah and assigned as a Unit of the newly established U.S. Indian Police Training and Research Center.

Under the Indian Offender Rehabilitation Program, counselors visited Federal and State prisons to help Indian prisoners make the best use of the available educational and rehabilitation programs within the institution and to help them plan for their release. The counselors arranged employment and education for prisoners who were about to complete their terms or be paroled. In some locations, Bureau of Indian Affairs personnel were the counselors. At other locations, the Bureau contracted the Indian organizations to conduct the program.

The Rehabilitation Center were multipurpose institutions designed to help both juvenile and adults who require detention. The Centers were in minimum security settings.

In 1966, the Major Crimes Act was amended to include carnal knowledge and assault with intent to commit rape. Both had been proposed in 1932 but rejected at that time. The addition of carnal knowledge was in response to a 1960 court decision holding that the term rape as used in the Major Crimes Act required a lack of consent and could not include statutory rape. In 1968, the law was again amended to include assault resulting in serious bodily harm. This amendment was passed as part of the Indian Civil Rights Act, which limited the sentencing power of tribal court to six months and a $500 fine. The Bureau believed that the punishment for an assault in which someone is seriously injured should be greater than six months in jail.

Another portion of the Indian Civil Rights Act provided for states that had assumed jurisdiction under Public Law 83-280 to return jurisdiction to the tribe and Federal Government with the mutual consent of all three parties. In 1971, the Omaha tribe in Nebraska was the first to secure the return of jurisdiction under this provision.

While individual Indians have long had the same rights in relation to State and Federal Governments as other citizens, several court decisions held that the restrictions found in the Bill of Rights and the Fourteenth Amendment did not apply to tribal governments. In 1968, Congress passed the Indian Civil Rights Act restricting tribal governments in most of the same ways Federal and State Governments are restricted by the Constitution. Federal Courts now review the actions of tribal police and courts when suit is brought alleging that rights protected by the 1968 law have been violated.

The law has put substantial pressure on the Indian Courts to improve their procedures to meet Constitutional standards. The year after the law was passed the National American Indian Court Judges Association was founded. The Association has sponsored three years of training programs for Indian judges using funds provided by the Law Enforcement Assistance Administration. The Association has also undertaken research into problems facing the Indian courts.

In mid-February, 1972, Raymond Yellow Thunder, an Oglala Sioux, was found dead in a truck several miles from the Pine Ridge Reservation. Fearing that the white youths who had killed him would go unpunished, about 1,000 Sioux lead by members of the American Indian Movement marched on the small off-reservation town where the perpetrators lived. A successful prosecution was forthcoming and an era of mass protests in Indian country began.

A year later came the two-month-long occupation of Wounded Knee that attracted world-wide attention. Before that event, there were a number of other mass protests. In order to cope with the higher potential for violence that necessarily accompanies mass protests, the Bureau organized the Special Operations Services Group (S.O.S.). The Unit is comprised of BIA officers who have been specially equipped and trained to deal with civil disturbances.

By 1974, the Bureau of Indian Affairs budget was $8,300,000. There were 342 BIA employees working in law enforcement. Tribes were employing 708 persons in the criminal justice system at a cost of approximately $5,000,000.

CONCLUSION

In the pre-reservation days, the failure of a tribal police society to carry out its duty would have meant the failure of the hunt for the whole tribe and raise the prospect of starvation. Today, the strength and health of Indian communities is no less dependent on the maintenance of safety and justice by Indian judges and law enforcement personnel.

The men and women who hold the gavel or wear the badge in the Indian Criminal Justice system today are charged with an awesome responsibility to carry on the work of those who came before. From Chief Spotted Tail of the Dakota's and Quanah, Chief Judge of the Kiowa Court, to Senator Gurney of South Dakota and the Honorable Warren E. Burger, Chief Justice of the United States Supreme Court, the importance of the Indian Criminal Justice system has long been recognized.

We must continue to improve the quality and efficiency of our work to better safeguard our communities and maintain the honor of our heritage.

Footnotes

[1] United States - Indian Office, Annual Report of the Commissioner of Indian Affairs (Commissioner's Report), 1869, p. 356.

[2] Ibid., p. 6.

[3] Com. Rep., 1872, p. 11.

[4] Ibid., p. 5.

[5] Com. Rep., 1873, p. 6.

[6] Com. Rep., 1874, p. 16.

[7] Com. Rep., 1872, p. 302.

[8] Com. Rep., 1873, p. 273 and Com. Rep., 1874, p. 307.

[9] William T. Hagan, Indian Police and Judges, (New Haven: Yale University Press, 1966) pp. 28-36.

[10] Loring Benson Priest, Uncle Sam's Step Children, (New Brunswick & Rutgers University Press, 1942) p. 139.

[11] Com. Rep., 1876, pp. IX-X.

[12] Com. Rep., 1877, p. 2.

[13] Ibid., p. 3.

[14] Hagan, op. cit., pp. 39-40.

[15] Ibid., p. 36.

[16] Com. Rep., 1881, P. XVIII.

[17] Com. Rep., 1874, p. 297.

[18] Ibid., p. 41.

[19] See e.g., Com. Rep., 1881, PP. 43, 193.

[20] Com. Rep., 1878, p. XVII.

[21] Com. Rep., 1880, pp. IX-X.

[22] Ibid.

[23] William MacLeod, "Police and Punishment Among Native American of the Plains," Journal of the American Institute of Criminal Law and Criminology, Vol XXVIII, 1937, pp. 182-184.

[24] Com. Rep., 1881, p. XVIII.

[25] Com. Rep., 1880, p. 2.

[26] Com. Rep., 1879, op. 36.

[27] Ibid., p. 42.

[28] Com. Rep., 1880, pp. 40-47.

[29] Ibid.

[30] Ibid., p. XI.

[31] Com Rep., 1881, p. XVII.

[32] Ibid., p. XIX.

[33] Com. Rep., 1882, p. 31.

[34] Ibid., p. 7.

[35] Hagan, op. cit., p. 57.

[36] Ibid., p. 58.

[37] Ibid., p. 59-68.

[38] Hagan, op. cit., p. 101.

[39] Com. Rep. 1888, pp. XXIX-XXX.

[40] Com. Rep. 1883, p. XV.

[41] Com. Rep. 1888, p. XXX.

[42] Com. Rep. 1886, p. XXVII.

[43] Com. Rep. 1883, p. 42.

[44] William T. Hagan, American Indians (Chicago, The University of Chicago Press, 1961) P. 138.

[45] Hagan, Indian Police and Judges, op. cit., pp. 89-145.

[46] Ibid., pp. 148-149.

[47] Ibid., pp. 112-113.

[48] Com. Rep., 1890, p. LXIII.

[49] Ibid., pp. 40-41.

[50] Hagan, Indian Police and Judges, op. cit., pp. 126-130.

[51] Ibid., pp. 134-135.

[52] Ibid., pp. 135-139.

[53] Com. Rep., 1892, p. 27.

[54] Hagan, Indian Police and Judges, op. cit., pp. 145-146.

[55] Ibid., p. 116.

[56] Ibid., p. 121.

[57] Ibid.

[58] Com. Rep., 1893, p. 191.

[59] Superintendent Forrest Stone, Letter to Commissioner of Indian Affairs, dated October 2, 1930.

[60] Com. Rep., 1897, pp. 57-58.

[61] Com. Rep., 1903, p. 35.

[62] Com. Rep., 1901, p. 51.

[63] Ch. 3504, 34 Stat. 325.

[64] Com. Rep., 1906, p. 41.

[65] Who Was Who in America, (Chicago: The A. N. Marquis Company, 1966), Vol. 2, p. 285.

[66] Victor Rousseau, "Pussyfoot," Harpers Weekly Advertiser, February 26, 1910, p. 548.

[67] Com. Reg., 1907, p. 34.

[68] Ibid., p. 32.

[69] Ibid.

[70] "Pussyfoot Got His Name," The Native American, February 10, 1923, p. 318.

[71] Com. Rep., 1907, p. 34.

[72] Ibid., p. 35.

[73] Com. Rep., 1908, pp. 34-35.

[74] Ibid., p. 38.

[75] Com. Rep., 1909, p. 14.

[76] Com. Rep., 1910, p. 12.

[77] Rousseau, op. cit., p. 549.

[78] Com. Rep., 1911, pp. 36-38.

[79] "Pussyfoot Johnson mobbed in London by Medical Students," The New York Times, November 14, 1919, p. 1, and "Johnson Becomes Popular Because of Taking Ragging Good Naturedly," The New York Times, November 15, 1919, p. 3.

[80] Com. Rep., 1912, p. 47.

[81] Investigation of the Indian Bureau, (Washington; U.S. House of Representatives Committee on Expenditures in the Interior Department, 1913), pp. 9-11.

[82] Com. Rep., 1913, pp. 13-14.

[83] Ibid., pp. 12-13.

[84] Com. Rep., 1913, pp. 12-14.

[85] Com. Rep., 1914, p. 43.

[86] Com. Rep., 1915, pp. 15-16.

[87] Indian Appropriation Bill: Hearings Before the Committee on Indian Affairs (Washington: 63d Con., 2d Sess., House of Representatives, December 9, 1914), p. 74.

[88] Indian Appropriation Bill: Hearings Before the Committee on Indian Affairs (Washington: 62d Cong., 2d Sess., House of Representatives, December 10, 1919), p. 105 and Indian Appropriation Bill: Hearings Before the Committee on Indian Affairs (Washington: 62 Cong., 2d Sess., House of Representatives, January 17, 1912), p. 55.

[89] Indian Appropriation Bill: Hearings Before the Committee on Indian Affairs (Washington: 64th Cong., 1st Sess., House of Representatives, December 20, 1915), pp. 27-29.

[90] Supra note 88.

Indian Law Enforcement History

[91] Indian Appropriation Bill: Hearing Before a Subcommittee of the Committee on Indian Affairs (Washington: 66th Cong., 2d Sess., House of Representatives, December 10, 1919), p.l 104.

[92] Interior Department Appropriation Bill: 1923, Hearing Before Subcommittee of House Committee on Appropriation (Washington: 67th Cong., 2d Sess., House of Representatives, December 14, 1921) p. 220.

[93] Interior Dept. Approp. Bill: 1928: Hearing Before Subcommittee of House Committee on Approp. (Washington: 69th Cong., 2d Sess., November 15, 1926) pp. 46-47.

[94] Indian Approp. Bill: Hearing Before a Subcommittee of the Committee on Indian Affairs (Washington: 65th Cong., 3d Sess., December 4, 1918) p,. 16.

[95] Interior Department Appropriation Bill, 1923: Hearings Before a Subcommittee of the House Committee on Appropriations (Washington: 67th Cong., 2d., Sess., December 14, 1921) p. 185.

[96] See e. g. supra note 93 at p. 48.

[97] Reservation Courts of Indian Offenses: Hearings Before the Committee of Indian Affairs (Washington: 69th Cong. 1st Sess., House of Representatives, Feb. 13 - May 20, 1926).

[98] Ibid., pp. 2-6.

[99] Ibid., pp. 18-29.

[100] Ibid., pp. 115-120.

[101] Ibid., pp. 121-141.

[102] Ibid., pp. 38-39.

[103] Ibid., pp. 86-88.

[104] Ibid., pp. 27-28.

[105] Int. Dept. Approp. Bill, 1926: Hearing Before Subcommittee of House Committee on Approp. (Washington: 68th Cong., 71st Sess., House of Representatives, November 21, 1924), pp. 716-718.

[106] Int. Dept. of Approp. Bill 1933: Hearing Before Subcommittee of House Committee on Appropriation: (Washington: 72d Cong., 1st Sess., December 19, 1931), pp. 225, 229.

[107] Supra note 93.

[108] Int. Dept. Approp. Bill for 1930: Hearing Before Subcommittee of House Committee on Appropriation: (Washington: 70th Cong. Sess., November 19, 1928) p. 717.

[109] Supra at note 106, pp. 229-230.

[110] Int. Dept. Approp. Bill for 1935: Hearing Subcommittee of House Committee on Appropriation: (Washington: 73d Cong. 2d Sess., December 21, 1933) pp. 426-430.

[111] S. Lyman Tyler, A History of Indian Policy (Washington: U.S. Department of the Interior, 1973) p. 131.

[112] Survey of Conditions of the Indians in the United States: Hearing Before a Subcommittee on Indian Affairs (Washington: 71st Cong., 3d Sess., U.S. Senate, May 28, 1931) pp. 11929, 11953.

[113] Interior Department Appropriations Bill, 1944: Hearings Before the Subcommittee of the Committees on Appropriations (Washington: House of Representatives, 78th Cong. 1st Sess., March 20, 1943) p. 41.

[114] Interior Department Appropriations Bill, 1936: Hearings Before a Subcommittee of the House Committee on Appropriations (Washington: 74th Cong., 1st Sess., February 7, 1935) pp. 687-696.

[115] Interior Department Appropriations Bill, 1937: Hearings Before a Subcommittee of the House Committee on Appropriations (Washington: 74th Cong., 2d Sess., December 19, 1935) p. 720.

[116] Missing from Original.

[117] Interior Department Appropriations Bill, 1938: Hearings Before a Subcommittee of the House Committee on Appropriations (Washington: 75th Cong., 1st Sess., April 6, 1937) p. 850.

[118] Supra note 115, p. 716.

[119] Interior Department Appropriations Bill, 1940: Hearings Before a Subcommittee of the House Committee on Appropriations (Washington: 76th Cong., 3d Sess., February 2, 1940) pp. 65-66.

[120] a. Interior Department Appropriations Bill, 1941: Hearings Before a Subcommittee of the House Committee on Appropriations (Washington: 76th Cong., 3d Sess., February 2, 1940) pp. 65-66.
b. Interior Department Appropriations Bill, 1948: Hearings Before a Subcommittee of the House Committee on Appropriations (Washington: 80th Cong., 1st Sess., February 12, 1947) p. 1318.

[121] Interior Department Appropriations Bill, 1944: Hearings Before a Subcommittee of the House Committee on Appropriations (Washington: 78th Cong., 1st Sess., March 20, 1943) p. 41.

[122] Supra note 113, p. 42.

[123] Interior Department Appropriations Bill, 1943: Hearings Before a Subcommittee of the House Committee on Appropriations (Washington: 77th Cong., 2d Sess., March 3, 1942) pp. 34-42.

[124] Supra note 120(b), pp. 1316-1318.

[125] Interior Department Appropriations Bill, 1949: Hearings Before a Subcommittee of the House Committee on Appropriations (Washington: 80th Cong., 2d Sess., February 24, 1948) p. 103.

[126] Interior Department Appropriations Bill, 1949: Hearings Before a Subcommittee of the Senate Committee on Appropriations (Washington: 80th Cong., 2d Sess., June 2, 1948) pp. 375-377.

[127] Interior Department Appropriations Bill, 1951: Hearings Before a Subcommittee of the Senate Committee on Appropriations (Washington: 81st Cong., 2d Sess., April 7, 1950) pp. 333-338.

[128] Interior Department and Related Agencies Appropriation for 1956: Hearings Before a Subcommittee of the Committee on Appropriations (Washington: Senate, 84th Cong., 1st Sess., April 7, 1955) pp. 649-651.

[129] Interior Department and Related Agencies Appropriation for 1957: Hearings Before a Subcommittee of the Committee on Appropriations (Washington: Senate, 84th Cong., 2d Sess., March 2, 1956) pp. 129-130.

[130] Department of Interior and Related Agencies Appropriation for 1960: Hearings Before a Subcommittee of the Committee on Appropriations (Washington: House of Representatives, 86th Cong., 1st Sess., February 3, 1959) p. 791.

[131] Interior Department and Related Agencies Appropriation for 1962: Hearings Before a Subcommittee of the Committee on Appropriations (Washington: Senate, 87th Cong., 1st Sess., April 25, 1961) pp. 188-189.

[132] Department of Interior and Related Agencies Appropriation for 1966: Hearings Before a Subcommittee of the Committee on Appropriations (Washington: House of Representatives, 89th Cong., 1st Sess., February 15, 1965) p. 759.

[133] Judicial Branch of the Navajo Nation--Annual Report for 1972 (Window Rock: Courts of the Navajo Nations, 1972) p. 3

Made in United States
North Haven, CT
17 April 2025